98.2   EDSC cl

Golding

DUCKS DON'T GET WET

Ducks Don't Get Wet

Ducks Don't

BY AUGUSTA GOLDIN

ILLUSTRATED BY

LEONARD KESSLER

THOMAS Y. CROWELL COMPANY · NEW YORK

Get Wet

LET'S-READ-AND-FIND-OUT SCIENCE BOOKS

Editors: *DR. ROMA GANS*, Professor Emeritus of Childhood Education, Teachers College, Columbia University

DR. FRANKLYN M. BRANLEY, Chairman and Astronomer of The American Museum–Hayden Planetarium

*AVAILABLE IN SPANISH

Copyright © 1965 by Augusta Goldin.

Illustrations copyright © 1965 by Leonard Kessler.

Manufactured in the United States of America

L.C. Card 65-11647

ISBN 0-690-24667-6   ISBN 0-690-24668-4 (LB)

5   6   7   8   9   10

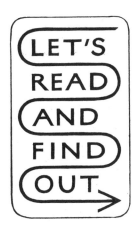
LET'S
READ
AND
FIND
OUT

Ducks Don't Get Wet

Ducks are water birds.

All day long, they go in and out of the water: in and
  out, in and out.

No matter how many times they go into the water, ducks don't get wet. Ducks are waterproof.

Every duck is waterproof because it has an oil gland near its tail.

With its broad bill, the duck strokes this oil gland. It smears the oil over its feathers. This is called preening.

Ducks spend hours preening themselves. This is how they keep their feathers covered with oil. Their feathers do not get wet because oil and water do not mix.

You can prove this for yourself.
Find some bird feathers in the woods.
Sprinkle water on one of the feathers. It will get wet
    because most bird feathers are not waterproof.

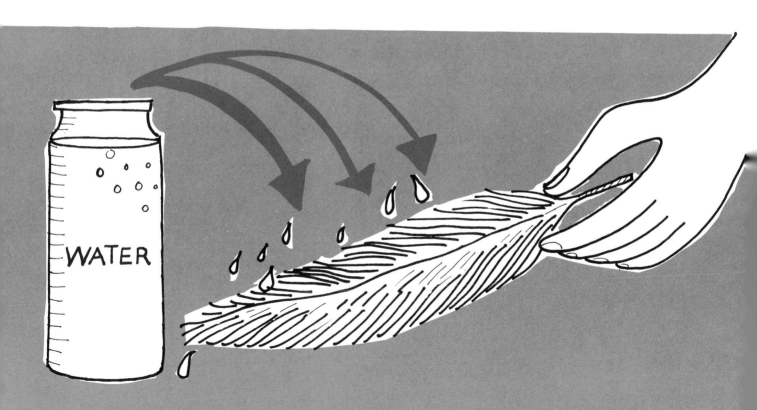

Dip your fingers in salad oil. Then pull a feather
through them. Do this two or three times. Now the
feather is coated with oil.

Sprinkle water on the oiled feather. The oiled feather
will not get wet because oil and water do not mix.

If you can't find any bird feathers, you can do another experiment to show that oil and water do not mix. Take two brown paper bags. Smear one paper bag with salad oil. Sprinkle water over both bags. The oiled paper bag will not get wet because oil and water do not mix.

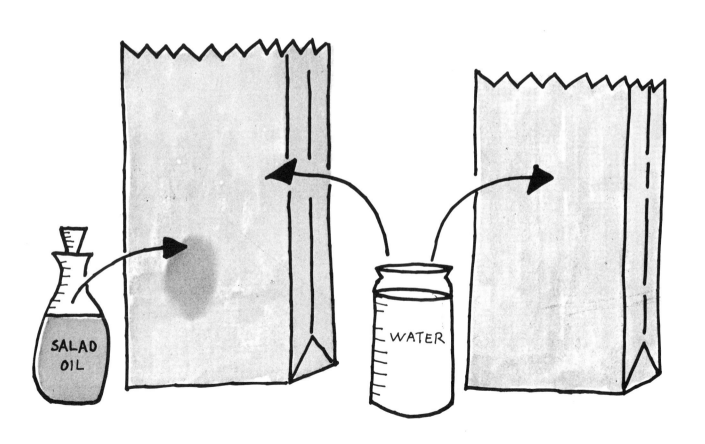

In the same way, water cannot get through the oil on
the feathers of a duck.

Ducks spend most of their time in the water.
They splash around in puddles and ponds, in swamps
and shallow streams. They tip up in ditches and
creeks. You can see ducks tipping their heads under
the water and tipping their tails up in the air.

When ducks dabble in the water, they are searching
  for food. Their webbed feet paddle fast as they tug
  waterweeds with their broad, yellow bills.
Pintail ducks and mallards search through the water
  for pondgrass and wild rice, for seeds and insects.

Blue-winged teals dip for wild rice and mussels, clams, crayfish and crabs.

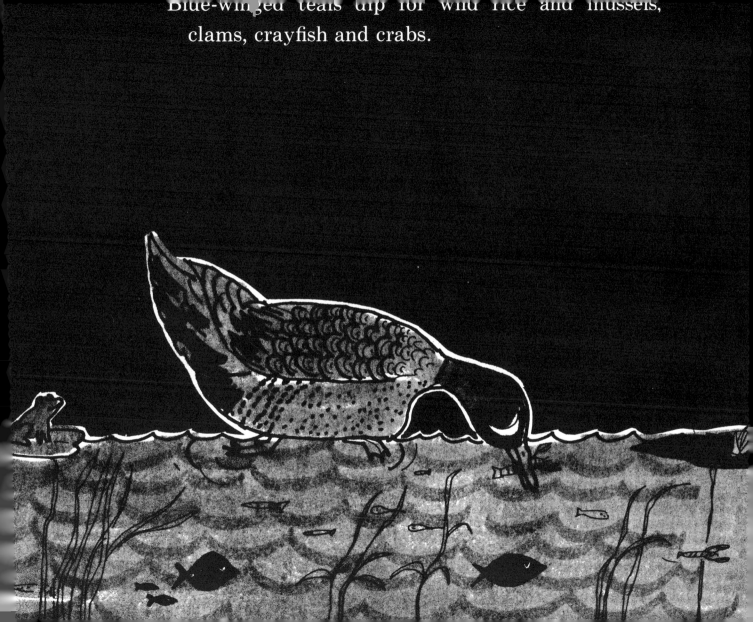

Shoveler ducks waddle in and out of shallow water. They shovel up mud and strain it for seeds and tiny water plants. They scoop up water and strain it for snails and insects, tadpoles and shrimps.

Wood ducks look for water plants. They eat duckweeds
and grass seeds, wild celery and lily seeds.

Many ducks are expert divers.
Some ducks can dive to the bottom of very deep lakes
and they will not get wet.

They can dive down 100 feet. This is as deep as a ten-story building is high. They can swim under water for 300 feet, the length of a city block. When they come up for air, they are dry.

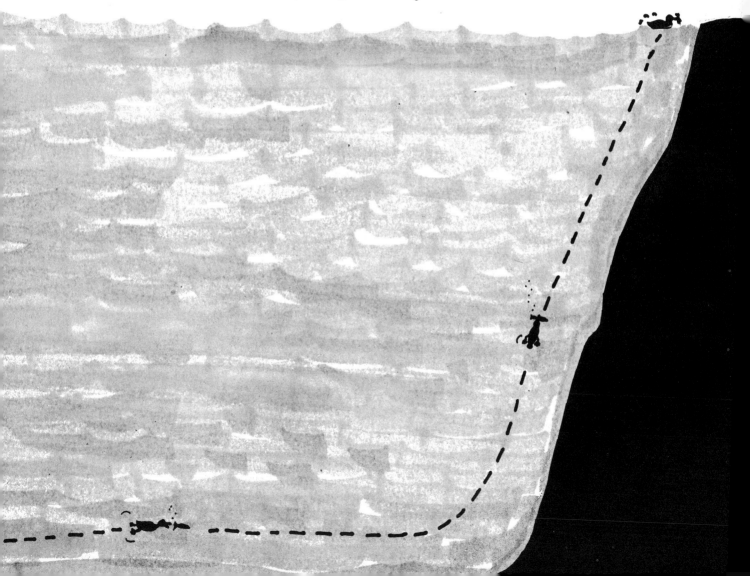

Harlequin ducks and canvasbacks dive for shellfish
and minnows.

Buffleheads and scaups dive for scallops and oysters and lobsters.

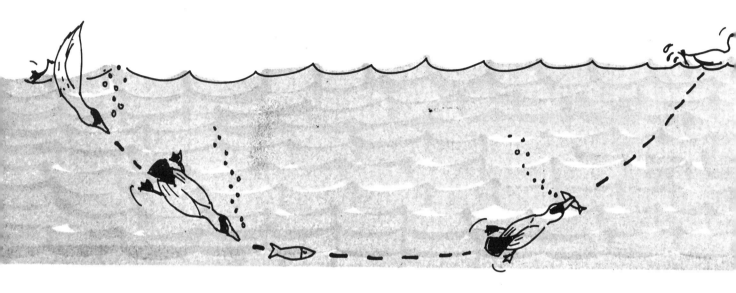

Eider ducks dive for blue mussels and worms, sea
urchins, sand dollars and small fishes.

Mergansers dive for large fishes. With its saw-edged
bill, a merganser can catch and hold a slippery fish.

Ducks must find their food in the water or along the shores of lakes and ponds.

When the weather gets cold, the rivers and marshes, ponds and lakes are covered with ice.

When the water freezes, crabs and crayfish, oysters and lobsters, duckweeds and pondweeds and all the fish are beneath the ice. Ducks cannot reach this good food.

Then the ducks leave the far north.
Then the ducks fly southward to open water where
  they can find food.

Southward fly the dabbling ducks:

the mallards and the pintails

the teals and the shovelers   and the wood ducks.

Southward fly the diving ducks:

the canvasbacks and harlequins

the buffleheads and scaups

the eider ducks

the mergansers.

Southward, at 50, 60, 70 miles an hour—as fast as a fast automobile—fly the ducks.

Southward to open water and good duck food fly the
ducks. They may fly through buffeting winds and
storm clouds. They may fly through sunshine and
slanting rain. And the raindrops roll right off their
backs.

If they fly over your house, you may be sure you will see them again next fall. Ducks travel the same route or FLYWAY year after year. Sometimes they fly in a V formation. The leader flies at the point of the V, and the other ducks fan out behind him.

When the ducks fly low, you may be able to see them clearly. You may be able to hear the hiss and whistle of the wind, as it slips off their oiled feathers. You may be able to hear the heavy thumping of their powerful wings.

But when the ducks fly very high, you will not be able to hear them, or to see a single duck. You will know that the ducks are passing overhead only when you see V's in the sky that look like faint wisps of smoke. You will know the ducks are flying southward for the winter.

When spring comes, the ducks will return.
They will fly north to dabble and dive in the rivers
and lakes, in the ponds and marshes.
They will fly back to open water and good duck food.

They will fly back north through blustering winds and
   spring rains.
And they will always be dry, because ducks don't
   get wet.

ABOUT THE AUTHOR

Augusta Goldin was born in New York City but grew up on a farm in the Catskill Mountains near Ellenville, New York. She was graduated from Hunter College, received a Master of Science degree from the City University of New York, and a doctorate of education from Teachers College, Columbia University.

Mrs. Goldin has worked on the staffs of several education publications and is the principal of a school on Staten Island, New York.

She has traveled around the world and visited Mexico, Canada, and Europe many times.

ABOUT THE ILLUSTRATOR

Leonard Kessler is well known not only as a children's book illustrator but also as a designer and commercial artist. He has a degree in fine arts, painting, and design from the Carnegie Institute of Technology.